MIRAGE!

Philippe Duchateau
& Salvador Mafé Huertas

Osprey Colour Series

MIRAGE!

DASSAULT'S MACH 2 WARRIORS

For Mercedes, who made this book and others possible

Published in 1990 by Osprey Publishing Limited
59 Grosvenor Street, London W1X 9DA

© Salvador Mafe Huertas 1990

British Library Cataloguing in Publication Data

Huertas, Salvador Mafe
    Mirage.
    1. Fighter Aeroplanes & attack aeroplanes.
Technical data
    I. Title
    623.74′64′0212

ISBN 0 85045 953 2

Editor Tony Holmes
Page design David Tarbutt
Printed in Hong Kong

Front Cover Tight formation flying at its best! Seemingly within touching distance, a weathered Mirage IIIBE of *Escadre de Chasse* 1/13 'Artois' formates with a sister aircraft from the same squadron during a training flight (*Philippe Duchateau*)

Back Cover A pair of veterans fly a neat two-ship over patchy cloud cover. Painted in the famous 'Fanta Can' scheme so long associated with this unit, the Mirage IIIO(F) and IIID belong to the Aircraft Research and Development Unit (ARDU), based at Edinburgh in South Australia. ARDU had the distinction of flying the last official RAAF Mirage sortie when A3-101, an ARDU IIID, was flown from Edinburgh to Woomera for storage on 8 February 1989 (*Greg Meggs*)

Title pages Cruising over the estuary-strewn coastline north of the squadron's home base at RAAF Williamtown, a No 77 Sqn Mirage IIIO(A) shows off its recently acquired tactical grey paint scheme. This particular Mirage ended its days flying with No 75 Sqn from Darwin and was flown to the Woomera storage facility in October 1988 (*Greg Meggs*)

Self-portrait of author Salvador Mafé Huertas flying back-seat in a Mirage CE.11/IIIDE, one of six operated by *Ala* 11, the *Ejército del Aire Espanol's* Mirage III wing. The highly stylized bone dome is even signed by the artist!

Similar angle, different author! Philippe Duchateau puts himself in the picture while riding back-seat in an *Armée de l'Air* Jaguar E. Flying alongside the Jaguar, but just out of shot, is a veteran Mirage IIIBE

Introduction

MIRAGE! presents a colourful *tour d'horizon* of all the operational versions of this quintessential family of French combat aircraft, with the single exception of the Mirage IV nuclear bomber. Not surprisingly, it is the Mirage III/5, one of the finest fighters to emerge from the 1950s, that forms the bulk of the photographic coverage in this book. An excellent selection of original photos illustrate aircraft from all around the globe.

Stunning air-to-air shots capture the Mirage in its element, up there amongst the whispy stratocumulus just itching for a dogfight with an unwitting adversary. Fly with the *Armée de l'Air* on a training sortie over southern France; prepare to 'mix it' with *Ejercito del Aire* Mirage F.1CEs in a two v two dogfight over the Iberian peninsula; and hold on tight as the crack crews from the South African Air Force scrape across the burnt veldt in search of enemy aircraft, proving that the Dassault delta is just at home 'in the weeds'.

The ultimate delta, the Mirage 2000, is also graphically illustrated, both fighter interceptor and nuclear penetrator variants being covered within this volume.

Enjoy the lavish colour schemes, matched only by equally lavish type designations, of the multifarious Mirage 5, the export bread winner for Dassault.

They are all here, each and every Mirage a fitting tribute to Dassault's brilliance as an aircraft designer *par excellence*.

Contents

The beauty of the Mirage III design is emphatically complemented by the dramatic dusk skyline. This particular delta silhouette belongs to *Escadron de Chasse 1/13 'Artois'* (*Philippe Duchateau*)

French finesse

Having trained its fair share of French aeronauts, a rather battered and faded Mirage IIIBE continues to ply the skies over France. Besides carrying two large drop tanks, a dummy Matra R. 550 Magic air-to-air missile is also bolted to the port outer wing hardpoint. This particular aircraft is employed by EC 1/13, the French Air Force's Mirage operational conversion unit (*Philippe Duchateau*)

Above A pair of Mirage IIIBs fly a tight formation over patchy banks of white cloud which have successfully obscured the Vosges mountains below. At the Mirage OCU pilots are taught all facets of flying the aircraft. Before being allowed to lead a formation like this one, the student pilot is instructed in the art of the wingman. A good wingman is able to 'stick' to his leader in combat, or while traversing through heavy cloud, and provide him with total fighter cover should a dogfight occur (*Philippe Duchateau*)

Left Flying towards the setting sun, a pair of Mirage IIIBs cruise over the Colmar region of southern France. Although an aircraft with a long history, the Mirage III is more than capable of mixing it with an experienced driver at the helm. The small cadre of frontline pilots have developed a complex series of manoeuvres which exploit the Mirage's rapid acceleration and 'point-and-shoot' capabilities to the fullest extent, allowing the aircraft to take on F-4s and Mirage F.1s with confidence (*Philippe Duchateau*)

Left Although sharing a common airframe, the Mirage IIIB differs markedly from its Dassault stablemate, the IIIBE. Developed to help pilots convert onto the brand new Mirage IIIC then entering service, the IIIB's basic fighter fuselage was lengthened by about two feet (60 cm) to accommodate a second seat. Because of its training role the fire-control radar was omitted from the nose section which allowed the Dassault designers to transfer all the electronics and radio equipment into the resulting space. The second seat was then fitted into the former equipment area. Similarly, the later uprated Mirage IIIE was

converted to dual seat configuration utilizing the E-models more powerful SNECMA Atar 09C, and the lengthened fuselage associated with this powerplant modification. Therefore, the Mirage IIIBE has a considerable edge over its older squadron mate in the thrust-to-weight stakes (*Philippe Duchateau*)

Above Using the tow bar as a convenient footrest, an EC 1/13 groundcrewman pauses to do up his bootlace. These two Mirage IIIBs are in the process of being prepared for the first sortie of the morning at Colmar air force base. The number 13 visible just forward of the crew

ladder refers to the 13th Wing (*Escadre de Chasse*), the parent unit of the OCU, while the two letters which make up the full code refer to the individual squadron and aircraft itself. A typical wing comprises three squadrons (*Escadrons*) which are usually named after French regions such as '*Artois*', '*Côte d'Or*', '*Ardennes*, and '*Alsace*' to name but a few (*Philippe Duchateau*)

Above With the wheels firmly chocked and the SNECMA Atar 09B slowly winding down, the groundcrewman approaches the recently returned Mirage IIIB carrying the crew ladder. A small yellow drum has been placed beneath the engine bay of the aircraft to catch any fluids which may leak from the powerplant after shutdown (*Philippe Duchateau*)

Right Being given the gouge about the rear cockpit of the Mirage IIIBE, Lieutenant Pierre Catto runs through the operational procedure for the inflight intercom with his instructor pilot. Being an officer under basic flying training at the *Ecole de l'Air*, Lieutenant Catto is taking advantage of the opportunity to get fast jet experience early on in his syllabus.

All trainee pilots are given this opportunity during their holidays, forgoing trips to the Riviera, St Tropez or contact with their family and friends. On the other hand they get to observe, absorb and talk frontline fast jets with fully qualified seasoned fighter pilots (*Philippe Duchateau*)

Above Gallic technology of the late 1950s at its best: the Mirage IIIBE front office is clinically simple, just as a fighter cockpit should be. No TV screens or on-board computer displays here; the pilot has to fly the aircraft, navigate it, visually check for enemy aircraft, and having successfully found his target, deliver his weapons through his own skill as an aviator. This is the best way for him to learn the job and fully appreciate new high-tech systems which proliferate in modern air force combat aircraft (*Philippe Duchateau*)

A pair of Mirage IIIBs leave Colmar on a routine sortie. *Escadre de Chasse 1/13 'Artois'* is the largest fighter squadron in the French Air Force, having two flights equipped with Mirage IIIEs and two with Mirage IIIBs and IIIBEs. The OCU flights were transferred to Colmar in July 1986 after their parent unit for many years, *Escadron de Chasse et de Transformation* (ECT) 2/2 *'Côte d'Or'*, re-equipped with the Mirage 2000B to continue its role as an OCU unit flying state-of-the-art equipment. Designated SPA 155 *'Petit-Poucet'* and

SPA 160 *'Diable Rouge'*, the Mirage IIIBs and IIIBEs should continue to form a substantial slab of EC 1/13's flying assets for a few years yet (*Philippe Duchateau*)

Right Staying in close to his leader, the wingman has lowered his aircraft's undercarriage and switched on the landing lights in preparation for a formation approach to Colmar. Although it has a notorious reputation for long and fast landing runs, a result of its delta wing configuration, experienced Mirage III pilots are able to land the aircraft in an amazingly short distance by deploying the braking parachute just before touchdown (*Philippe Duchateau*)

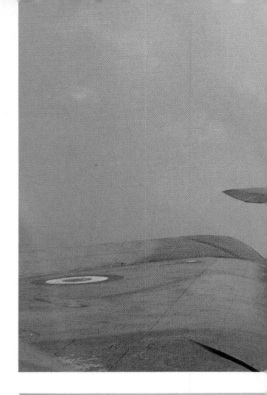

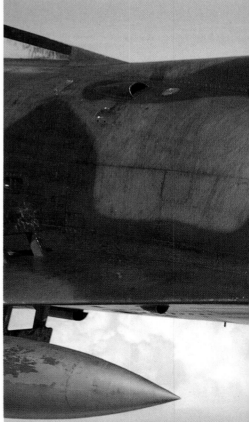

Right A lovely close-up of the trainee pilot and instructor at work in their airborne office. The generally well-worn appearance of the IIIB is typical for an aircraft that flies on virtually 365 days a year. The physical proportions of the canopy itself are quite generous and give the crew virtually unlimited vision (*Philippe Duchateau*)

Most flights undertaken by EC 1/13 see the Mirages carrying a pair of small supersonic drop tanks to help extend the flying time available to instructors and students (*Philippe Duchateau*)

Left and overleaf The Mirage in its element. Returning from a 1 v 1 dogfight out of Colmar, the 'enemy' of the sortie manoeuvres behind the Mirage IIIB to allow Philippe Duchateau to capture these memorable images

Screaming out for a good polish, a bare metal Mirage IIIBE of ECT 2/2 'Côte d'Or' soaks up the sun at Dijon. This unit has since passed its two-seaters onto EC 1/13 and re-equipped with Mirage 2000Bs (*C Boisselon*)

Fully bombed up the prototype Mirage 5 taxies out across a very damp runway to begin yet another test flight in late 1967. Essentially an austere Mirage III, the 5 (initially known as Mirage V) was developed especially for the Israeli Air Force (IDFAF) following their experiences in combat flying the Mirage IIICJ. Utilizing the airframe and engine of the Mirage IIIE, the Dassault designers dispensed with the expensive interception radar and moved all the remaining electronics into the nose, following the pattern set by the trainers. The resulting space was used for an extra internal fuel tank. Two additional weapons pylons were installed, making seven in all, and these could carry up to 4000 kg (8820 lb) of weapons and 500 lt (220 gal) of fuel during ground-attack missions. Fifty Mirage 5s were ordered by Israel as the 5J but they never reached the Middle East as the De Gaulle administration embargoed their delivery in June 1967 (*J Cuny*)

Although almost 20 years old, this Mirage 5 looks virtually brand new. In fact this aircraft has only a nominal number of flying hours under its belt, having just been returned to service after spending the best part of its life hidden from the elements at Châteaudun Air Base. Now attached to EC 3/13 'Auvergne', the aircraft flies daily from Colmar. After the embargo on exports to Israel was imposed the 50 completed Mirage 5s were stored at Châteaudun until 1971 when the French and Israeli Governments agreed upon a financial settlement which saw the aircraft purchased for the *Armée de l'Air*. Redesignated Mirage 5Fs, they were subjected to a rigorous weapons and tactics trials programme before being issued to EC 3/13, a squadron especially formed to operate these surprise acquisitions (*Philippe Duchateau*)

Right Celebrating the squadron's 15th anniversary since its formation in May 1972, this flashy Mirage 5 added a splash of colour to EC 3/13's ranks for several months in 1987 (*C Boisselon*)

Below Another special commemorative scheme developed for the anniversary, but this time worn on an aircraft from a different flight. For some reason the airbrakes are deployed on this particular Mirage 5
(*via Salvador Mafé Huertas*)

Overleaf Along with operating the Mirage III/5 OCU, EC 1/13 '*Artois*' is also a veteran Mirage IIIE user. They first received C-model Mirages as F-86K Sabre replacements in early 1962, assigned to the air defence duties of *Commandement Air des Forces de Défense Aérienne* (CAFDA). In 1965 the squadron re-equipped wth the multi-role Mirage IIIE and its assignment switched to the close-air support tasking of the *Forces Aériennes Tactique* (FATac). With its tail resembling a medieval battle flag, an '*Artois*' Mirage IIIE was liberally daubled with patriotic colours to celebrate the thirtieth anniversary of the Wing's association with Colmar Air Base (*C Boisselon*)

Sitting on the ramp at Cambrai during the 1979 Tiger Meet, a weary Mirage IIIE of EC 3/2 'Alsace' takes a break from exercise commitments. A veteran Dassault squadron, EC 3/2 flew Mystère IVAs until Mirage IIICs started replacing them in December 1961. After serving CAFDA for almost a decade the squadron traded in their C-model Mirages for the more capable E-model, and were reassigned to FATac accordingly. Like many other Mirage III squadrons, EC 3/2 finally retired their venerable mounts in favour of the vastly superior Mirage 2000C in the mid 1980s, returning to CAFDA at the same time (*G Grondstein*)

Carrying an interesting assortment of tanks and weapons on its stores pylons, a Mirage IIIE of EC 2/4 'La Fayette' cruises at height over Luxeuil Air Base. Arguably the *Armée de l'Air's* most famous fighter squadron, the *Sioux Escadron* was originally formed at Luxeuil (still its current base) on 18 April 1916 as *'l'Escadrille Américaine N124'*. Formed almost entirely from American volunteers, the deeds of EC 2/4 during the First World War are legendary. *'La Fayette'* squadron received its first Mirage IIIEs in October 1966, replacing the well worn Republic F-84F Thunderstreak. Configured here to perform the vital low-level nuclear strike role tasked to the unit in 1972, this Mirage IIIE has an AN.52 tactical bomb, two large fuel tanks and a solitary PHIMAT chaff pod hung beneath its slender delta wings. The squadron performed its last operational sortie with the IIIE on 10 November 1988, raking up a total of 160,000 flying hours over 22 years of service. The two-seat Mirage 2000N now wears the proud 'Screaming Sioux' on its tail (*AMD-BA*)

Left Fully kitted up with navigation maps and check lists tucked into his G-suit webbing, Captain Borel of *Escadre de Chasse Tous Temps* 30, the F.1 OCU, checks the underside of his mount during his pre-flight walkaround. Borel is a very experienced Mirage F.1 driver, being fully qualified as a patrol leader. During his walkaround check the pilot looks for any unsecured panels, inspects recent maintenance work and ensures that no hydraulic fluid or fuel is leaking from his aircraft (*Philippe Duchateau*)

Preceding pages Parked side by side in a blast pen at Colmar Air Base, these two Mirage 5Fs belong to EC 3/13 '*Auvergne*'. All 50 Mirage 5Fs were modified to French standards by the Air Force maintenance unit at Châteaudun (*via Salvador Mafé Huertas*)

Above Surrounded by various ground auxiliary units and carrying a pair of long-range ferry tanks beneath its wings, this Mirage III is of the reconnaissance variety. A total of 50 recce Mirages were acquired by the French between 1961 and 1965, serving exclusively with *Escadre de Reconnaissance* 33 at Strasbourg Air Base. Utilizing the Mirage IIIE airframe, five Omera cameras were fitted into the specially lengthened nose bay of the IIIR. Unlike most other reconnaissance aircraft, the Mirage IIIR retained its combat capability. This particular Mirage IIIR wears the striking tail markings of ER 1/33 '*Belfort*', a unit now equipped with the far more capable Mirage F.1CR (*C Boisselon*)

Above Wearing a scheme not entirely representative of a typical recce Mirage, this glossy black aircraft was specially decorated to mark the end of ER 3/33 '*Moselle's*' 25-year association with the IIIR and IIIRD. The squadron changeover to the Mirage F.1CR also coincided with ER 3/33's 90,000th hour of flying the veteran Mirage III. This particular Mirage was one of 20 IIIRDs built to supplement the earlier recce aircraft, these later machines having a far superior navigation, camera control and infra-red tracking suite (*C Boisselon*)

Right Completing the arduous task of suiting up before a back-seat familiarization flight in an ECTT 3/30 Mirage F.1B, Captain Francois Debost straightens out a restraining strap before clipping it to his G-suit webbing. Captain Debost is an engineering graduate from '*L'Ecole Polytechnique*', one of France's most prestigious universities. He attended the '*Sup Aero*' after graduation to improve his aeronautical engineering knowledge, before undertaking pilot training at the '*Ecole de l'Air*' and completing his course as a fighter pilot. He will eventually continue his career as a flying engineer at the famous Istres Test Centre, working on the Rafale project (*Philippe Duchateau*)

Left During the late 1960s and early 1970s Dassault investigated ways of improving the low-level manoeuvrability of the Mirage III/5 series by fitting fixed or moving foreplanes to the nose of the aircraft. Known as the *Milan* (Kite), three conversions were made; a Mirage 5J in September 1968, a Mirage IIIR in May 1969 and a Mirage IIIE, which was re-engined with an Atar 09K-50 and flew for the first time in May 1970, christened the Milan SO.1. The costs of the programme were shared with the Swiss, who were looking at supplementing their already substantial Mirage III fleet with additional aircraft. However, they opted for the Northrop F-5E Tiger II despite the vastly improved low-speed performance of the 'moustachioed' Mirage. This low down shot of the Milan SO.1 clearly shows the foreplanes in their extended position, as well as the Aida radar ranging unit specially mounted in the converted nose of the aircraft (*AMD-BA*)

Below The wing layout may be different, but from virtually any angle the Mirage F.1 shows definite signs of its Mirage III lineage. Displaying the effectiveness of its air superiority blue/grey tactical scheme, this F.1C belongs to *Escadre de Chasse* 5 based at Grange Air Base, but is seen here briefly stopping in at Salon (*Philippe Duchateau*)

Right Proving that French fighter pilots are as good as any at the cool long steely stare, Captain Borel 'checks his six'. The visible slope of the SEM Martin-Baker F10M ejection seat helps the pilot pull sustained G without blacking out (*Philippe Duchateau*)

Below Soon to prove his mettle in a one v one dogfight over his home base of Reims-Champagne, Captain Borel checks his front office before engine fire-up (*Philippe Duchateau*)

Left All set for combat, Captain Debost gives the traditional thumbs-up. Being a seasoned fighter pilot by the time he begins work on the Rafale, Debost will be able to impart his experience as both a technician and a flyer to the overall development programme (*Philippe Duchateau*)

Below 'Visor versa'! Staring into the early morning sun, the instructor pilot consults his groundcrew visually before releasing the brakes and taxiing out. Above his head is the canopy-shattering cordite charge which will detonate automatically should the pilot have to punch out of his aircraft (*Philippe Duchateau*)

Tightly strapped in, the pilot cranes
his neck from side to side in order to
spot his adversary and avoid being
jumped. Reflections from buckles and
other metallic objects are a constant
distraction to the pilot's highly
sensitive eye (*Philippe Duchateau*)

Above Virtually devoid of external stores, a Mirage F.1B banks over a solid mass of undulating cloud. *Escadre de Chasse Tous Temps* 30, in accordance with their operational conversion role, was the first wing to receive the F.1C, declaring themselves operational on 5 July 1974. Originally flying the single-seater only, the wing eventually received the training-optimized F.1B (*Philippe Duchateau*)

Overleaf Unlike the Mirage IIIB and BE the Mirage F.1B retains the full fighter radar fit, mounting a Thomson-CSF Cyrano IV fire-control system in the nose which gives it an all-aspect, all-altitude interception capability. The B-model does however lose the integral DEFA 553 30 mm cannon and some fuel capacity. The seeker head of an inert Matra R.550 Magic missile and the perforated airbrake fitting snugly beneath the fuselage can both be seen in this close formation shot (*Philippe Duchateau*)

The small tail badge hardly merits a mention on this ECTT 3/30 'Lorraine' F.1B, a far cry from the flamboyantly decorated fins of ten years earlier. The dummy R.550 Magic AAM has a fully operational seeker head fitted to it which allows the pilot to operate the missile accurately in conjunction with the fire-control radar during practice dogfights with other similarly-equipped squadron aircraft (*Philippe Duchateau*)

Close formation flying in tactical fighters is not to be recommended in a combat situation. However, the art of formation flying is a valuable asset to any potential combat pairing of wingman and leader, and is taught relentlessly throughout pilot training all over the world. Stability and relative positioning are vital when flying close, these techniques being taught to potential fighter pilots on Fouga Magisters during their initial fast jet training. Vertical separation during tight manoeuvring is also essential. The concentration involved during the initial teaching of these techniques is so intense that exhaustion can sometimes set in. Having completed their scheduled dogfighting the instructor-piloted Mirage F.1s close ranks for some formation work (*Philippe Duchateau*)

Left Wearing a scheme conspicuous by its sheer unsuitability to European operations, these two F.1CRs are part of a small batch of aircraft specially sprayed in these temperate colours for operations in Chad. Attached to ER3/33 '*Moselle*' and ER 1/33 '*Belfort*' respectively, these aircraft fly in support of *Operation Epervier* (Sparrowhawk) out of N'Djamena International Airport. The multi-role nature of the F.1CR has been exploited to its fullest in Chad, the recce aircraft usually flying sorties with interceptor F.1C-200s (*C Boisselon*)

Below The final variant of the Mirage F.1 series to enter service was the reconnaissance dedicated F.1CR, the first squadron being declared operational on type in September 1983. Retaining full combat capability like the earlier Mirage IIIR, the F.1CR has two optical OMERA cameras fitted and a SAT SCM 2400 Super Cyclope infra-red detector in the cannon bay. The aircraft can also carry a variety of exotic radar and photographic pods on its centreline pylon. With a camera blister clearly visible beneath the squadron code, a weathered F.1CR from ER 3/33 '*Moselle*' taxies out at Salon (*Philippe Duchateau*)

Above Photographed at its home base of Orange-Caritat, this freshly sprayed F.1C belongs to EC 2/5 'Ile-de-France'. Fully loaded-up, it carries a 1200 litre centreline tank, an R.550 Magic on each wingtip and a Super R.530 long range air-to-air missile under each wing, all the missiles painted blue to signify that they are dummy rounds. Along with sister squadron EC 1/5, 'Ile-de-France' has since converted onto the Mirage 2000C/RDI (*C Boisselon*)

Top right The ultimate delta fighter, the elegant Mirage 2000 features all the classic Dassault design traits. Painted in patriotic house colours, the original prototype Mirage 2000.01 is now a highly prized exhibit at the Le Bourget Aerospace Museum. The aircraft was built in a record 27 months at St Cloud and flew on 10 March 1978 at Istres (*Philippe Duchateau*)

Right Looking absolutely pristine, this Mirage 2000C belongs to EC 3/2 'Alsace' and was photographed at its home base, Dijon-Longvic. Fitted with a Thomson-CSF/Electronique Marcel Dassault pulse Doppler radar, this particular aircraft, and many other new build 2000s, has finally been united with the originally proposed system which has suffered such a long gestation period (*C Boisselon*)

Waving the flag as unofficial NATO members, a pair of Mirage 2000Bs from ECT 2/2 'Côte d'Or' sit side by side on the 40th anniversary ramp at the 1989 Mildenhall Air Fete. From this angle the beefed-up spine associated with the two-seater is clearly visible (*Tony Holmes*)

With the canopy left slightly open to help him keep his cool, a pilot from ECT 2/2 awaits the signal from his groundcrew which will allow him to taxi out onto the runway. The heat haze emanating from the variable aspect exhaust nozzle signals that the SNECMA M53-2 turbofan is fully spooled up (*Philippe Duchateau*)

Left Head down, concentrating on his throttle quadrant, a Mirage 2000 instructor prepares to depart on a brief sortie over Mildenhall to practise his airshow routine. The refuelling probe to the left of the canopy is detachable, Dassault prefering not to build an integral receptacle into its fighters (*Tony Holmes*)

Right The striking camouflage scheme worn on all CAFDA Mirage 2000s enhances the already flattering lines of the aircraft. As with all Mirage fighter designs of the past, the dedicated two-seater did not materialize until well into the 2000 project. Last of the officially-funded prototypes, but first to full production Mirage 2000C standard, airframe number 04 first flew from Istres on 12 May 1980 (*Tony Holmes*)

Preceding pages A two-seater with a difference, the Mirage 2000N is the latest variant of Dassault's fighter family to enter service. Optimized for the low-level nuclear penetration role, the 2000N has replaced the venerable Mirage IIIE in squadron service. The airframe on this version has been strengthened to allow the crews to fly the aircraft at very high speeds at heights down to about 200 feet. The 2000N is also packed with state of the art French electronics including the ESD Antilope V terrain-following radar, two Sagem inertial platforms, an improved radio altimeter and special ECM gear. Both cockpits are fully equipped with CRT (cathode ray tube) displays (*Philippe Duchateau*)

Preceding page Waiting for the *Patrouille de France* to finish their practice display in the azure Suffolk skies, the Mirage 2000 pilot sits baking in the warm May sun on the taxiway. The elegantly styled helmets that are unique to the *Armée de l'Air* have two separate visors, the tinted one being most appropriate in this instance (*Tony Holmes*)

Above One of three 2000Ns assigned to the *Centre d'Expérimentations Aériennes Militaires* (CEAM), this aircraft is configured in the typical low-level strike mode. The jumboised drop tanks beneath the wings give the aircraft an impressive combat radius. The small white dog on the aircraft's tail is the emblem of EC 3/530 (*C Boisselon*)

Total procurement of the Mirage 2000 family for the French Air Force is currently expected to be between 300 and 400 aircraft, 112 of these being N models. The ASMP medium-range air-to-surface nuclear missile is the 2000N's major weapon, although ten non-ASMP aircraft have been built to fulfil conventional attack roles until the Rafale is available in the early 1990s. This particular aircraft, seen at Metz, belongs to EC 1/4 *Dauphine*, the first squadron to convert onto the 2000N, an event which took place at Luxeuil in July 1988 (*Philippe Duchateau*)

Antipodean aeronauts

A sight which is sure to evoke many fond memories for Australian aviation enthusiasts! Flying at height in the hazy skies over Malaysia, a trio of Mirage IIIO(A)s from No 79 Sqn prepare to pitch out and recover at RAAF Butterworth. The fifth, and last, Mirage III squadron formed to operate the Dassault fighter, No 79 Sqn stood up in 1986 at Butterworth. A Sabre squadron in the 1960s, No 79 had been disbanded in Thailand in 1968, and was reformed in Malaysia 18 years later to replace No 3 Sqn who were leaving Butterworth for Williamtown and the new F/A-18 Hornet. With the withdrawal of the RAAF from Butterworth in 1988 came the end of No 79's brief association with the Mirage, the squadron once again being disbanded (*Greg Meggs*)

The distinction of being the last operational Mirage IIIO unit in frontline service with the RAAF went to No 75 Sqn, the 'Magpies' also having the distinction of being the first Mirage IIIO squadron in the RAAF, forming up on the type in 1965. Having put in many years of service in defence of the 'great southern land', Mirage IIIO(A) A3-96 is now stored, pending sale, at Woomera in South Australia. Partly covered in tarpaulins, the aircraft is seen at Pearce Air Force Base in Western Australia during No 75 Sqn's last deployment with the Mirage to the west in September 1987 (*Tony Holmes*)

The 1980s brought a new appraisal of combat aircraft markings the world over, the RAAF following the trend and low-vising a substantial number of Mirages in air superiority grey. However, the fin flash and the distinctive kangaroo roundel remained as a testament to past schemes. With its exhaust nozzle cover laying face down on the Pearce ramp, A3-60 awaits the final finishing touches from the No 75 Sqn boys before being lowered off the jacks (*Tony Holmes*)

Overleaf To commemorate the passing of the Mirage from RAAF service No 75 Sqn resprayed A3-33 in period 1965 colours, the aircraft contrasting markedly with its squadron mates (*RAAF*)

Inset Repainted in the scheme it would have worn when delivered from the Avalon factory in February 1966, A3-33 had the distinction of flying the final operational sortie of No 75 Sqn with the Mirage in September 1988. All Mirages were delivered to the RAAF in this scheme up until January 1967, the remaining 50 IIIOs entering service in the standard French Air Force dark green and slate grey, a scheme eventually worn by the whole Mirage force. Like all good Mirages, this airframe is now reposing in a shed at Woomera awaiting sale (*RAAF*)

Below Twelve months before it was resprayed, A3-33 is seen heading a line-up of No 75 Sqn aircraft basking in the early morning sun at Pearce Air Force Base in September 1987. Up on jacks, A3-33 is 'Atarless', the squadron groundcrew effecting a quick powerplant change before the day's flying commences (*Tony Holmes*)

Flying a tight six-ship formation over Darwin, No 75 Sqn pilots show off their prowess as aviators for the benefit of the camera. Carrying the standard pair of supersonic drop tanks on each aircraft, the closest trio also carry dummy R.550 Magic AAMs on the outboard wing pylons (*RAAF*)

Looking suitably pensive, Wing Commander Bill Evans ponders his future after completing his final flight in a Mirage IIIO. Tasked with ferrying A3-23 from Darwin to Woomera for storage, the Wing Commander would have had plenty of time during the flight to mull over his long career in the Mirage (*Greg Meggs*)

Bottom right Carrying a squadron leader's pennant and a pair of R.550 Magic AAM dummy rounds, A3-54 of No 77 Sqn taxies out at Ohakea Air Base in New Zealand in October 1984. Nicknamed the 'Grumpy Monkeys' because of their squadron badge, a Korean lion, No 77 Sqn was formed in 1942 in response to the Japanese bombing of Darwin, and flew P-40 Kittyhawks throughout the 'island hopping' campaign that dominated the war in the Pacific. Part of the occupation force sent to Japan after the war, the squadron re-equipped with the P-51 Mustang, which they took to war over Korea. Eventually becoming part of the jet age in 1951, No 77 Sqn specialized in close-support ground attack work with their new mount, the Meteor F.8. After three years of war the squadron returned home to Williamtown. The Meteors were phased out in 1956 when the Avon-Sabre Mk 32 began to appear in numbers. In 1959 the unit joined fellow Sabre operators No 3 Sqn at Butterworth in Malaysia, a relationship that was to last almost ten years. The Mirage IIIO entered No 77 Sqn service in June 1969, the 'Grumpy Monkeys' remaining based at Williamtown with the Dassault fighters until converting to the F/A-18 in July 1987 (*Greg Meggs*)

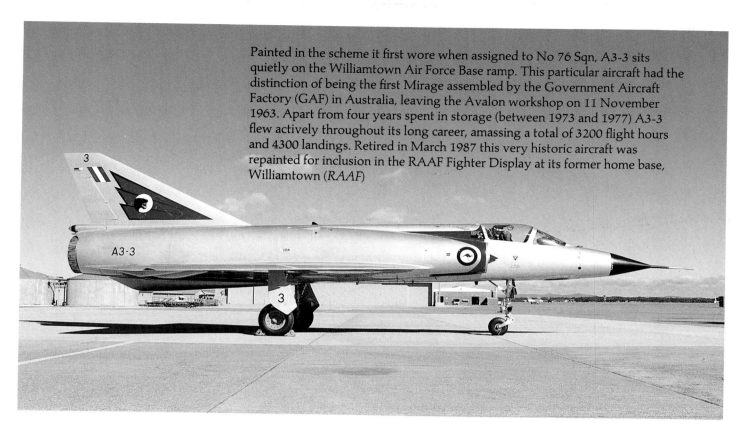

Painted in the scheme it first wore when assigned to No 76 Sqn, A3-3 sits quietly on the Williamtown Air Force Base ramp. This particular aircraft had the distinction of being the first Mirage assembled by the Government Aircraft Factory (GAF) in Australia, leaving the Avalon workshop on 11 November 1963. Apart from four years spent in storage (between 1973 and 1977) A3-3 flew actively throughout its long career, amassing a total of 3200 flight hours and 4300 landings. Retired in March 1987 this very historic aircraft was repainted for inclusion in the RAAF Fighter Display at its former home base, Williamtown (*RAAF*)

Looking suitably spotless on the Williamtown ramp, A3-80 is in fact the squadron CO's aircraft, the special tail markings denoting this. Although equipped with a standard Mirage IIIO nose, this aircraft was one of a small number converted to mount a special reconnaissance radome. The Cyrano radar was removed on these aircraft and a Fairchild KA-56-BI panoramic camera fitted in its place. An optional camera pack could also be mounted in the gun bays in place of the twin DEFA 30 mm cannon. Designated Mirage IIIO(PR), all of these converted airframes were flown by No 77 Sqn (*Greg Meggs*)

Although never the mount of the
official RAAF aerobatics display
team, several Mirage IIIs from No 77
Sqn received the special treatment in
1981 during the RAAF's Diamond
Jubilee celebrations. This particular
aircraft, A3-72, hasn't yet received
the finished 'nose job', the radome
eventually being painted blood red.
The other two machines to receive
this treatment were A3-15 and A3-48
(*Gregs Meggs*)

Right Once a No 76 Sqn aircraft, A3-12 ended its flying days with the Air Research and Development Unit (ARDU) at Edinburgh Air Force Base in South Australia (*Greg Meggs*)

Below Climbing out from Williamtown, a Mirage student pilot commences another training sortie. A total of 192 Atar 09C3/03Z engines were ultimately supplied to the RAAF, 140 of them being built by the Commonwealth Aircraft Corporation between 1964 and 1969 (*RAAF*)

Although totally devoid of squadron markings this Mirage IIIO(F) belonged to No 2(F) Operational Conversion Unit, based at Williamtown. The delta fighter's high approach and landing speed meant bad news for the Mirage's braking system, and a deployable parachute was fitted to the aircraft to help slow the machine down after touchdown. After a brief stint with the OCU, A3-34 ended its squadron service flying with No 79 Sqn at Butterworth. Together with 49 other Mirages, the aircraft is now cocooned at Woomera
(*Greg Meggs*)

The RAAF eventually received 16 Mirage IIIDs to help in the training of future Mirage pilots, this particular aircraft being the last Mirage built to the original Air Force order, although six additional machines were delivered from Avalon to meet training requirements in 1973. With a red aggressor band applied to the fuselage, this No 2 OCU machine is being pre-flighted by the crew before the mission commences. The OCU disbanded in 1984 and reformed a year later as the F/A-18 conversion unit, the Mirage training role passing on to No 77 Sqn. This Mirage IIID eventually ended up with No 79 Sqn at Butterworth, and up until its final flight to Woomera, had knocked up almost 3000 hours of flying time (*RAAF*)

The extended nose and underfuselage strakes are clearly visible on this No 2 OCU Mirage IIID as it performs a touch-and-go at Williamtown (*RAAF*)

With the mandatory RAAF-issue tin dustbin strategically placed beneath the engine of the aircraft to catch fluid leaks, a No 75 Sqn Mirage IIID sits quietly in the static park during the 1986 Pearce Airshow. Several of the twin-seat Mirages were resprayed in the tactical grey scheme, the drab paint weathering markedly in the humid Darwin weather (*Tony Holmes*)

Pictured at Darwin on 30 September 1988, the day in which the Mirage III was finally retired from frontline service, Mirage IIID A3-113 sits alongside a No 75 Sqn mate on the ramp. Beneath the white vinyl cover is a Martin-Baker Mk 4B ejection seat (*RAAF*)

Mirage Europe

High above the rugged Spanish countryside a pair of Mirage IIIEEs from *Escuadrón* 112 prepare to mix it with a brace of *Ala* 14 Mirage F.1CEs during a dissimilar air combat training sortie. A total of 24 Mirage IIIEEs and 7 IIIDEs were purchased by Spain in 1970, equipping *Escuadróns* 111 and 112, both part of *Ala de Caza* 11 which is based at Manises, near Valencia. Piloting the lead Mirage in this two-ship formation is Captain Gutierrez, his wingman on this occasion being Captain Nuñez. The wingman's machine is equipped with a dummy AIM-9P3 Sidewinder AAM (*Salvador Mafé Huertas*)

Carrying two F2 rocket launchers and a pair of empty RPK bomb launcher/fuel tanks beneath its wings, an *Escuadrón* 112 aircraft returns from a weapon's delivery sortie. The surviving 16 Mirage IIIEEs and five IIIDEs are soon to be upgraded in an extensive programme formulated by Israeli Aircraft Industries. Internally a new AN/AYK-14 mission computer linked to a digitalized 1153 data bus, AN/APQ-159 multimode radar and laser inertial navigation system is being fitted. A flare/chaff dispenser and new IFF equipment also form part of the upgrade, as does a digital weapons management system. Externally, four new stores stations have been added, a single pressure refuelling point fitted, plus an air-to-air refuelling probe. A forward fuselage plug has been fitted in front of the cockpit to allow the added avionics to be housed in the slender Mirage airframe. An extra internal fuel tank has also been added behind the cockpit (*Salvador Mafé Huertas*)

The elegant delta planform of Dassault's classic fighter can be appreciated from this angle as two Mirage IIIEEs fly together in a tight combat formation. Painted white, the Marconi Doppler navigation equipment bulges can also be seen underneath the forward fuselage of both aircraft (*Salvador Mafé Huertas*)

Overleaf Showing its age, a rather worn Mirage IIIEE from *Escuadrón* 111 banks over the deep blue waters of the Mediterranean. The major reason for the Mirage update is the smaller than predicted order placed by the Spanish Air Force for the F/A18 Hornet, budgetry restraints reducing it from 144 to just 72 aircraft. The predicted threat from well-equipped north African countries was also considered when the update was proposed (*Salvador Mafé Huertas*)

Right Wearing his personalized helmet, Captain Rafael Nuñez glances down from his lofty perch as the aircraft's crew chief peers inside the port intake following a test flight after an engine change. This close-up of the nose reveals just how battered the paintwork on the Spanish Mirages really is! (*Salvador Mafé Huertas*)

Below The pilot guides his Mirage IIIEE down onto Runway 30 at Manises, the aircraft descending forcefully at about 170 knots (*Salvador Mafé Huertas*)

From one NATO member to another. Wearing earthy camouflage well-suited to its task, a Mirage 5BR of the Belgian Air Force's *42e Escadrille/Smaldel* sits unobtrusively amongst other NATO aircraft at the 1989 Mildenhall Air Fete. The Belgians received a total of 106 Mirages of various marks, 22 of them being optimized to fulfil the tactical reconnaissance role like this aircraft. Although the strike Mirage 5BAs of the Belgian Air Force are rapidly disappearing as more F-16 Fighting Falcons enter service, the recce 5BRs are scheduled to soldier on into the next century, with only minimal avionics and airframe upgrades planned (*Tony Holmes*)

Right A Mirage operator that is forging ahead with its updating programme is Switzerland—this particular airframe serving as the evaluation aircraft. Approved by the government in 1985, the Improved Swiss Mirage Aircraft (ISMA) programme is being undertaken by F + W, the government's official

Above Based at Bierset, this lavishly decorated Mirage 5BA was painted up in mid 1987 to celebrate the 70th anniversary of *1ère Escadrille*. The intended Mirage Update Programme (MUP) has been delayed by the Belgian government until the early 1990s because of budgetry cuts in defence spending, although for added pilot safety the Martin-Baker Mk 10 zero-zero seat has been retrofitted to all surviving Mirages (*C Boisselon*)

aircraft establishment for research, development, production, maintenance and modification of military aircraft and guided missile systems. The Swiss Air Force currently operates 52 Mirage IIIs of various marks, most of which are to be updated. Airframe changes include the fitting of non-moving canards, slim strakes beneath the nose of the Mirage, wing refurbishing and a general rework of the airframe. The canards vastly improve the aircraft's manoeuvrability and low-speed handling, while the strakes increase the Mirage's stability near the edge of its flight envelope. Internally, a new Martin-Baker Mk 4 seat has been fitted, as has an infra-red/passive/active ECM suite. This particular aircraft first took to the air in this form on 23 August 1983. The ISMA programme is expected to be completed in 1990 (*Swiss AF*)

Wearing a very worn overall light grey paint scheme, this Mirage IIIS belongs to *Fliegerstaffel* 16, based at Stans. The Swiss Mirages have a two-position nosewheel strut which, when extended, lowers the tail of the aircraft and allows it to fit inside *Kavern* hangars, shelters that have been built into sheer rock faces. Constructed in the 1950s for the shorter Hunter, the *Kaverns* are virtually impregnable to 'iron' bombs (*C Boisselon*)

Right Flying over terrain that could only be Swiss, a *Fliegerstaffel* 10 recce Mirage IIIRS banks towards the camera. The Swiss acquired 18 reconnaissance optimized Mirage in 1968/69, the surviving airframes being modified during the IMSA programme. An Omera camera battery is mounted in the nose of the aircraft, and a Hughes Taran 1S navigation/attack system provides the pilot with precise directional details (*Swiss AF*)

Above Emphasizing the duality of their role, an *Flf Stff* 10 Mirage IIIRS taxies in after completing a sortie armed with a pair of AIM-9P Sidewinder missiles. Together with the two dedicated Mirage IIIS interceptor squadrons, the Swiss recce unit regularly deploys to the warmer Air Combat Range at Deci, on the Mediterranean island of Sardinia, for dissimilar air combat training (DACT) (*C Boisselon*)

Top right A total of 36 Mirage IIISs were acquired by the Swiss, with the first two being built in France by Dassault in early 1964. The remaining 34 aircraft were built by the Federal Aircraft Works at Emmen between October 1965 and February 1969. Up to 100 Mirages were originally on order but major cost overruns forced a drastic cut in this figure. Belonging to *Flf Stff* 16, this Mirage IIIS is carrying both AIM-9P Sidewinders and a centrally mounted Aérospatiale AS-30 air-to-surface missile (*C Boisselon*)

Right Firmly tethered to the runway, the pilot fires up the internally-mounted SEPR 841 rocket during a ground test at Emmen. Providing a thrust of 1500 kilograms, the engine has a total running time of just 80 seconds, although it can be switched on and off as required by the pilot. The Swiss regularly mount JATO bottles to their Mirages. This particular aircraft was the second Dassault-built Mirage IIIS, and it served as the nav/attack system trials aircraft at Holloman Air Force Base in the USA during the mid 1960s. It has spent the best part of the last decade at F + W undertaking various testing work (*F + W*)

The granddaddy of all Swiss Mirages dominates this busy view of the F + W factory at Emmen. Wearing the serial J-2201, this Mirage was acquired by the Swiss Air Force in December 1962 as a trials aircraft. Built as a IIIC, this machine was the only C-model Mirage operated by the Swiss, spending its entire service life with the Department of Flight Testing at Emmen before being retired to the Swiss Air Force Museum in 1981 (*F + W*)

Dassault rarities

A sight which emphasizes the popularity of the Mirage III/5 with nations across the globe. Altogether over 1400 first-generation Mirages were produced by Dassault, or manufactured under licence. Two-thirds of these aircrafts were exported, four customers being present in this colourful line up at Dassult's test facility at Bordeaux-Mérignac. Heading this unique gathering is a Mirage IIIEA of the Argentine Air Force, followed by a Libyan Mirage 5DR, a Pakistani Mirage 5PA, two Venezuelan Mirage 5Vs, another Libyan 5DR and alongside, a Pakistani 5PA (*via Salvador Mafé Huertas*)

Below Virtually brand new, a spotless Argentine Mirage IIIDA is checked out by Dassault engineers in June 1972. Soon after this photo was taken this Mirage was loaded into an Argentine Hercules and flown to South America. The first of two dual-seat Mirages delivered to Argentina, I-001 was written off in March 1979 during a training sortie (*via Salvadore Mafé Huertas*)

Right Snugly fitted into his Mirage IIIEA, a pilot from *Grupo 8 de Caza* taxies out before commencing another patrol of the Argentine coast during the Falklands conflict. This particular aircraft was one of the original 10 IIIEAs supplied to Argentina in 1972 (*via Salvador Mafé Huertas*)

Below Possibly the last time the whole squadron was together, pilots of *Grupo 6 de Caza* pose in front of one of their IAI Daggers during the Falklands conflict in 1982. A virtual carbon copy of the Mirage 5, the Dagger was produced by the Israelis after the French government placed an embargo on military hardware sales to that country following the 1967 Six Day War. Powered by the Atar 09C engine, the Dagger served with the Israelis for over a decade, 36 refurbished aircraft eventually finding their way to Argentina in 1978. Photographed the day after it had participated in a raid on Royal Naval vessels south of Port Stanley, C-412 survived the Falklands conflict and is still in operational service today (*via Salvador Mafé Huertas*)

Left To help make up numbers after the losses sustained by the Argentineans in the Falklands, Peru supplied 10 Mirage 5Ps from their own stocks in June 1982. Seen in this line up at Tandil Air Base, the 5Ps are on strength with *Grupo 6*, nine aircraft remaining out of the 10 supplied. These aircraft, like the Daggers before them, are currently being updated, this basically consisting of the fitting of an Argentine nav/attack system known as '*Mara*' to the aircraft at the Rio Cuarto Air Depot (*via Salvador Mafé Huertas*)

Below left Seen on a stormy day at Dassault's Melun-Villaroche facility, a factory fresh single seat Mirage IIIEA sits alongside a specially marked Mirage IV in April 1972. Almost twenty years later this Mirage IIIEA is still flying with the *Fuerza Aérea Argentina* and has recently been repainted in a new air superiority blue scheme which more befits its role (*via Salvador Mafé Huertas*)

Below Taxiing beneath the name of the man himself, a sleek Mirage IIIDBR destined for Brazil departs on a pre-delivery test flight, the dayglo orange flight suits of the Dassault test pilots clearly visible in the large cockpit. Designated the F-103D in Brazilian service, this Mirage was one of four two-seaters ordered by the *Forca Aérea Brasileira* in 1970, 12 single-seat IIEBRs (F-103Es) being despatched to South America as well. A further six Mirages (three F-103Es and two F-103Ds) were bought in 1978 as attrition replacements, all Mirages serving with 1 and 2 *Esquadrones* of 1 *Grupo de Difesa Aérea* at Anapolis (*via Salvador Mafé Huertas*)

While work is carried out on the nosewheel strut, a Dassault test pilot glances casually across at a Mirage that is slightly larger than the one he is currently strapped into. Wearing the rather complex roundel of the *Fuerza Aérea Colombiana*, this Mirage 5COA was one of 14 built as replacements for the Canadair Sabres of *Grupo Aéreo de Combate* 1. Two reconnaissance 5CORs and a pair of 5COD trainers were also built, deliveries taking place between September 1971 and July 1973 (*via Salvador Mafé Huertas*)

As new as they come! The sun glints off of a freshly constructed Colombian Mirage 5COD in October 1971. After a drawn-out negotiation period, the surviving Mirage 5s are to be joined by 13 Israeli Kfir C7/TC7 aircraft surplus to that nation's requirements, and IAI will perform a limited upgrade on the French built machines (*via Salvador Mafé Huertas*)

Carrying a pair of large drop tanks beneath its wings, a camouflaged Mirage 5COA banks over the French countryside during a test sortie in October 1971. All Colombian Mirages are based at German Olano Air Base, with regular detachments sent to Barranquitta and San Andres (*via Salvador Mafé Huertas*)

Seen high over south-west France, a Venezuelan Mirage 5DV formates for some publicity photography during an acceptance flight in 1973. The *Fuerza Aérea Venezolanas* received 10 Mirage IIIEVs, four Mirage 5Vs and a pair of Mirage 5DVs, all of which went to *Escuadrones* 33 and 36 of *Grupo Aéreo de Combate* 11 at El Libertador Air Base. Attrition has taken its toll on the original 16 aircraft and only ten remain in frontline service, although they are to be upgraded to Mirage 50 standard, which includes the fitting of canards. A further 12 ex-French Air Force Mirage IIIEs are also to be upgraded to this standard and delivered to Venezuela (*AMD-BA*)

The smallest order for the Mirage III/5 came from the ex-French colony of Gabon, a small nation in western Africa. Three Mirage 5Gs and two Mirage 5DGs were delivered in 1978 but unfortunately two were lost soon after in a mid-air collision. Originally, two recce 5RGs were also on order but these were cancelled due to lack of funds. Following a visit to Gabon by President Mitterrand of France in January 1983 an agreement was reached whereby four Mirage 5Gs and two 5DGs were supplied to the small African country. Designated Mirage 5G-IIs, the first of their number arrived in 1984 (*AMD-BA*)

Marked with the distinctive Saudi Air Force roundel, this Mirage 5SDD was in fact destined for Egypt, being one of 38 Mirages ordered by the oil-rich Saudis in September 1973. Orders for further Mirage 5s came directly from Cairo, another 44 aircraft eventually being delivered (*via Salvador Mafé Huertas*)

Framed by the unmarked tail of a Peruvian Mirage 5DP, a hybrid Mirage 'IIIE/5SDE' squats on the flightline, the victim of a comprehensive hydraulics failure. This particular aircraft is in fact a Mirage IIIE that was originally destined for the French Air Force. Three single-seaters and three two-seaters were pulled from the Bordeaux-Mérignac production line and, as can be seen here, completed as Saudi/Egyptian aircraft. When this photo was taken in October 1975 the Saudi roundel was only partially completed, the green disc giving the aircraft a temporary Libyan flavour (*via Salvador Mafé Huertas*)

Also carrying incomplete Saudi markings, one of six Mirage 5SDDs ordered in the initial batch is seen before delivery in June 1975 (*via Salvador Mafé Huertas*)

The Libyan Mirages were painted up at Dassault in an identical scheme to the Saudi/Egyptian aircraft, the first of 15 5DD trainers seen here departing on an acceptance sortie in October 1970, three months before it was delivered to Dijon for instructional use. A total of 110 Mirage 5s were eventually purchased by Libya, the surviving aircraft sharing Gemal Abdel Nasser Air Base with the more recently acquired Mirage F.1s (*via Salvador Mafé Huertas*)

Showing off its underbelly during a tight turn, this Libyan Mirage 5DE wears French roundels on its wings. This aircraft, equipped with both Cyrano and Doppler, was one of a batch of 32 5DEs delivered to Dijon and used to train Libyan pilots on type before eventually being flown to North Africa. With the Doppler bulge beneath the chin of the aircraft and the conical Cyrano-laden radome, these Libyan Mirages were essentially E-models in every sense bar the designation! (*via Salvador Mafé Huertas*)

Soon to operate the Mirage 2000, the Air Force of the United Arab Emirates has over 18 years experience flying Dassault deltas. A total of 29 Mirage 5s of several marks were delivered to Abu Dhabi, the major contributor of military hardware in the United Arab Emirates. This suitably camouflaged machine is a recce optimized 5RAD, one of three delivered in 1976. Along with the survivors of a dozen Mirage 5AD attack aircraft delivered in 1974, the RADs are assigned to No II Shaheen Sqn based at Al Dhafra (*via Salvador Mafé Huertas*)

Framing an Egyptian Mirage 5SDE
on the test ramp, the Dassault test
crew complete their final preflight
checks on a Mirage 5DM destined
for the *Force Aérienne Zairoise*. A total
of 17 Mirage 5s were procured by
Zaire in 1975, a far smaller number
than was originally planned. Of the
three Mirage 5DM trainers originally
delivered only one now survives
(*via Salvador Mafé Huertas*)

Above The early morning sun highlights the rather unusual two-tone green camouflage scheme applied to all the Mirages destined for Zaire. This particular 5DM was the second trainer built for the African nation (*Salvadore Mafé Huertas*)

Above right Parked alongside a Fouga CM.170 Magister, a spotless Mirage 5M sits awaiting its pilot. This airframe was the first of 14 single-seaters delivered to Zaire, only seven of which remain in front line service with *211e Escadrille*, part of the *21e Wing de Chasse et d'Assaut* at Kamina (*via Salvador Mafé Huertas*)

Right The Mirage has been the workhorse for many air forces over the past three decades, performing virtually any task thrust upon it. One nation however has not got its money's worth out of the Dassault fighter. In 1965 the prosperous Lebanese ordered 10 Mirage IIIELs and two IIIBLs for their emerging Air Force. Unfortunately civil war enveloped the country just as the Mirages were arriving in the Middle East and five of their number were immediately placed in storage. Sporadically flown alongside the surviving Hawker Hunter F. 70s, two Mirages have been lost in accidents over the past two decades. Stored for the best part of the last eight years, the Mirages have been periodically offered for sale or exchange, and are probably in unserviceable condition (*via Salvador Mafé Huertas*)

In contrast to the Lebanese, one country that has got more than its money's worth out of the Mirage is South Africa. One of the initial customers for the aircraft, the South Africans eventually received a total of 58 Mirages of no less than seven different marks! Firing a salvo of unguided rockets from both of its JL-100 combined fuel tank and rocket pods, a Mirage IIID2Z from No 85

Air Combat School lets loose on the firing range below. The number 2 in the aircraft's designation signifies that this trainer is one of eight surviving Atar 9K-50 powered Mirages, 11 of which were delivered in 1972. The five other Mirage two-seaters assigned to the Combat School are IIIBZ and DZ trainers powered by the significantly less punchy Atar 09B (*H Potgieter*)

Right Climbing into the vertical, an unmarked Mirage IIICZ of No 2 Sqn goes hunting armed with a pair of locally produced Kukri infra-red homing AAMs mounted under the wings. The Kukri has been modelled around the Matra Magic missile and has proved its effectiveness in combat over Angola (*H Potgieter*)

Preceding pages Based at Pietersburg, this Mirage IIID2Z carries a dummy AIM-9B Sidewinder round on the outer wing pylon. Involved in a one v one combat sortie, both pilot and instructor scour the clear blue southern African skies for a glimpse of their adversary. Recently a Mirage IIID2Z was the first of its type rebuilt to Cheetah standards by Atlas Aircraft. The Cheetah is essentially a Kfir C7 with an Atar 09K-50 engine fitted in place of the venerable General Electric J79. Fitted with canard foreplanes and an advanced South African radar and fire control suite, all 46 surviving Mirage IIIs are to be refurbished to Cheetah standards, with Atlas having the capacity to build brand new aircraft if the need arises (*H Potgieter*)

Below Flying over scrubland near the precarious border shared with Mozambique, this No 2 Sqn Mirage IIICZ is one of 14 survivors out of the original 16 delivered to the squadron at Waterkloof Air Base in December 1962. Coded number 800, the aircraft is in fact the very first South African Mirage built by Dassault. The beautifully balanced fuselage of the C-model Mirage is perfectly illustrated by this superb photograph. The battle-seasoned pilots of No 2 Sqn are based at Hoedspruit, close to the Mozambiquean border, and are ready to intercept any straying MiG-17 or MiG-21 aircraft that may penetrate South African airspace (*H Potgieter*)

Still wearing French style green and grey camouflage, one of four Mirage IIIR2Zs delivered in the early 1970s blasts off from the Waterkloof runway in full afterburner. Joining four previously delivered IIIRZs on strength with No 2 Squadron, the recce Mirages have flown extensively at high and low level over the heavily defended Angolan scrublands during South Africa's long war with that country. One IIIR2Z was lost to ground fire over Angola during such a mission in 1979, this being the only loss, admitted by the Air Force, of a first-generation Mirage during the whole Angolan conflict (*H Potgieter*)

Besides the Mirage IIICZ the most
common first-generation delta in
service with the Air Force is the
IIIEZ, 17 of which were delivered
between 1965 and 1972. Assigned to
the Air Combat School, whose badge
can be seen at the top of the fin, this
Mirage IIIEZ has its large braking
parachute deployed to help arrest its
progress down the Pietersburg
runway. Once the aircraft has slowed
sufficiently the pilot will release the
parachute and taxi in to dispersal.
Denoting that it has just returned
from an ACM training sortie, a single
dummy Sidewinder round is attached
to the port wing pylon (*H Potgieter*)